A SEARCH to my BEGINNING

An inspirational adoption story told through poetry, illustrations, and reflections.

Written by
JOAN BATTILANA

© 2003 by Joan Battilana. All rights reserved.

No part of this book may be reproduced, stored in a retrieval system, or transmitted by any means, electronic, mechanical, photocopying, recording, or otherwise, without written permission from the author.

ISBN: 1-4107-0551-X (E-book)
ISBN: 1-4107-0552-8 (Paperback)
ISBN: 1-4107-0553-6 (Dust Jacket)

Library of Congress Control Number: 2002096729

This book is printed on acid free paper.

Printed in the United States of America
Bloomington, IN

Illustrated by: Brenda Mattson
Edited by: Janet Johns

1stBooks – rev. 01/16/03

DEDICATION PAGE

To my Mom and Dad, Peg and Bill Schleisman:
For their unconditional love and support.
Thank you for choosing me; I don't know where I'd be.

To my biological Mother, LaJean Smith:
For her unselfishness, courage, and strength.
Your choice was hard to make.

To my husband Mark, whom I love dearly:
For standing beside me as I searched to my beginning.

To my sisters, Jill and Karen, and to my brother John:
For accepting our many differences while growing up.
And for understanding my reasons for searching.

To my entire biological family:
For accepting that we are a family by chance and friends by choice.

And finally, to my son Matthew:
For sharing his opinions with me.
And especially for the true mother-son bond that we share.
I love you Matt.

TABLE OF CONTENTS

PREFACE vii

A SEARCH TO MY BEGINNING 1

IN THE WOMB 5

BIRTH MOTHER'S CHOICE 9

"MY ADOPTIVE PARENTS" 13

ADOPTION WAS THE ANSWER 17

YOUR ARMS 21

THE CALL 25

ME! THE ADOPTEE 29

WHAT ADOPTION IS TO ME 33

HAPPY FATHER'S DAY! 37

MY MOM 41

THIS MOTHER'S DAY 45

HE NEVER KNEW 49

OUR BLENDED FAMILY 53

"FAMILY BY CHANCE"	57
DIFFERENT	61
"THAT BIG BROTHER OF MINE"	65
MY LITTLE BROTHER	69
"SISTERS BY CHANCE"	73
OUR BABY	77
'REUNION DAY'	81
I'M GLAD I FOUND YOU	85
SOME THOUGHTS TO REFLECT UPON	88

PREFACE

If you are the adoptee, have you ever wondered why the choice of adoption was made for you? Do you question what your life would have been like if you were not adopted? Or maybe, did you ever wonder whom you look like or wonder why you act the way you do? Rejection, does that thought ever enter your mind?

If you are the adoptive parents what questions have entered your mind? Maybe why your adopted child has different thought patterns or acts differently than you, even though you raised them from birth? Are you fearful that you child will want to search for and find his/her birth family?

If you happen to be a birth parent, do you have regrets? Do you wonder, worry, or cry about the child you gave up for adoption? Do you have hopes and dreams of one day finding that child? Does your life seem empty because someone is missing?

Many of the questions have or may at some point in time surface. For me, an adoptee, the questions and feelings did not surface until I was forty. My husband and I were watching a made for television movie one evening in June after my fortieth birthday. The movie was about a birth mother searching for her son that she had given up for adoption. As we watched, tears ran down my face and I had a strong desire to search to my beginning. That desire did not go away, it continually nudged at me. Questions were entering my mind and I had no answers. I knew the only way to have them answered was to begin searching. And that is just what I did.

I had concerns as I began my search, what if I found my birth family and I was rejected or what if I never found them. Most adoption files are sealed and they are difficult to open. But I took my chances. I started my research; I worked day and night on the computer for bits and pieces of information. Timing is everything. I know God places certain people at specific times in their lives to help direct and guide. I remember calling the hospital I was born in and asking the woman that answered the phone if she could fax me my birth record. (I had an advantage because I knew the day, date and time I was born). Without hesitation the woman faxed me the information. On the sheet was the name of my birth mother. If I would not have called at that very moment in time, I know without a doubt, I would never had received that important piece of information. The woman, who I know was an angel sent from God to help me, should not have sent me the name. It is confidential information, especially when an adoption has occurred. I did call back to the hospital one week later after finding my birth mother to thank this woman for sending me the last piece to my puzzle. The person that answered the phone said they have never heard of the woman I was looking for. She was not or had not been an employee of the hospital. Chill bumps still rise when I think about what happened.

My search was successful, which I am thankful for. The adoptee in me truly surfaced during my search and my discoveries. A talent I never knew I had appeared. Poems began to flourish, I could not write them down fast enough. Feelings entered my mind that I never realized existed. Questions I had never thought to ask were suddenly being answered through my poetry.

I sincerely hope the following pages of poetry and illustrations will shed some light on areas you are having difficulties with whether you are an adoptee, an adoptive parent, or a birth parent. The reflection pages are for your inner thoughts and feelings. Each time you read the pages new feelings will surface as they do each time I read them.

A SEARCH TO MY BEGINNING

Forty years have gone by
I began to wonder why,
I was born to a mother
And given to another.
The questions began to arise, how, when and who?
God had the original plan and He truly knew!
I prayed for answers and looked for clues,
God sent me an angel, who had good news.
The name of the woman who had to choose.
I picked up the phone and dialed her number…
Surprise!! Do you remember?
Through tears of gladness and tears of pain,
I learned that I truly gained.
Forty years was a long time past,
Decisions were made for my life to last.
Gladly, I began my search, regretful I am not
My beginning discovered and I have learned a lot.
My search ends not here as I go forward without fear
I know in my heart, God truly had His part.

Joan Battilana

A Search to my Beginning

Gladly, I began my search, regretful I am not
My beginning discovered and I have learned a lot.

Joan Battilana

A Search to my Beginning

IN THE WOMB

I am in the womb and what do I hear?
Decisions are being made because my arrival is near.
Adoption? Why does this have to be?
Why is this being chosen for me?
I don't know why this happened,
I am so very frightened.
Am I naughty or being rejected?
I thought I was in here being protected.
You've waited nine months for me to be born
How can you now seem so torn?
I promise I'll be good; I won't be much trouble,
I'll smile a lot and stay out of rubble.
The family has been chosen
Thank God, I won't be an orphan.
This all seems so unjust
Who can I learn to trust?
Why was I put up for adoption?
Apparently, you had no other option.

Joan Battilana

A Search to my Beginning

**I am in the womb and what do I hear?
Decisions are being made because my arrival is near.**

Joan Battilana

BIRTH MOTHER'S CHOICE

Words cannot express the feelings I have inside,
I carry a baby and have to decide.
Should I keep this precious gift or say good-bye?
All I seem to do is pray and cry.
What kind of life would this baby live?
A single young mother does not have much to give.
The love for this baby will grow and grow
Oh God! I just don't know.
Termination is not an option,
I think the choice should be adoption.
I want to find a family who is loving and kind
For I am having to leave my baby behind.
They will raise my baby to be their own,
I will step back and leave them alone.
It is now time to say good-bye
I will wonder, worry, and cry.
This choice of mine was hard to make
But I had my baby's life at stake.

Joan Battilana

**The choice of mine was hard to make
But I had my baby's life at stake.**

Joan Battilana

A Search to my Beginning

"MY ADOPTIVE PARENTS"

The only parents I have ever known,
They could have no children of their own.
A call was made one day in June
A daughter would arrive real soon.
A woman gave birth to a little girl,
Whose hair had only one little curl.
The woman's decision was tough to make,
But made my parents' hearts no longer ache.
The day arrived when the little girl became their own,
They finally had their little gemstone!
Joan is the name they chose for me
They'd wipe my nose and bandage my knee.
Not a day went by without giving thanks to the Lord,
For it was by His good graces their prayers were not ignored.
What a blessing my parents have been,
They've been there through thick and thin.
Mom and Dad is who they will always be.
They have given there ALL to me.

Joan Battilana

**Mom and Dad is who they will always be
They have given there all to me.**

Joan Battilana

A Search to my Beginning

ADOPTION WAS THE ANSWER

Years went by and we gave up the fight
Timing for us never seemed right.
We tried and we tried to have a baby of our own
That was not part of the plan God had sewn.
We heard about adoption
And wondered if that would be our option.
We prayed to hear the laughter of a child
So we went right down and filed.
There must be a baby out there
Who needs love and someone to care.
We got a phone call early one day
Are you ready? Your daughter is on her way.
Nervous and excited we couldn't wait to see.
Mommy and Daddy is who we will be.
When we finally laid our eyes upon her
We knew adoption had always been the answer.

Joan Battilana

**We heard about adoption
And wondered if that would be our option.**

_____
_____
_____
_____
_____
_____
_____
_____
_____
_____
_____
_____

Joan Battilana

A Search to my Beginning

YOUR ARMS

A phone call one day was all the notice
The child you waited for was ready for closeness.
Your arms opened and welcomed me
You did not even know who I'd be.
Your arms held me as your own
I know they'll be there when I am grown.
God had chosen your arms for me
He knew parents you were ready to be.
Your arms have made me feel safe and secure
They always seemed to have the cure.
Thankful I am each and every day
For your arms have loved me and showed me the way.

Joan Battilana

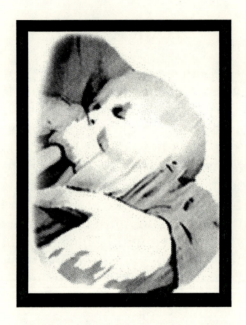

A Search to my Beginning

**Your arms held me as your own
I know they'll be there when I am grown.**

Joan Battilana

A Search to my Beginning

THE CALL

I placed a call to Mom and Dad one day,
There was something I had to say.
Forty years have come and gone,
I am so grateful for all you have done.
I am just curious and I want to know,
Who was the family that let me go?
Would it hurt you or make you mad,
If I found them and felt glad?
Do not worry my love for you is not at stake
I just need to know for my own sake.

Joan Battilana

A Search to my Beginning

**I placed a call to Mom and Dad one day
There was something I had to say.**

Joan Battilana

ME! THE ADOPTEE

Me! The Adoptee, how proud I am to be.
I have always known I was adopted
No reason to hide or be disappointed.
I was given a life I may never have known
By a young woman who was on her own.
Unselfish she was to give me life then let go
To a family who desired a child to love and watch grow.
Throughout the years I have always felt blessed
Even though God has put me to the test.
My family never made me feel different
Their love and care was always significant.
Many asked me in all the years past,
"Aren't you curious to know? We just have to ask."
In earlier years I never did care
But now that I am older I wonder if I dare,
Search for the woman who decided to let go
So I can thank her and let her know
That I am the Adoptee and so proud to be.

Joan Battilana

A Search to my Beginning

Me! The Adoptee, how proud I am to be.

Joan Battilana

What Adoption is to Me

Adoption makes one mother happy, yet one mother sad
It gives a child a life she may never have had.
Adoption is love,
Sent from up above.
A simple decision, adoption is not
A baby is let go, but never forgot.
Adoption prevails
When all else fails.
Adoption is why many have smiled
For without it they could not have a child.
Answers to adoption are not easy to find
Especially when you leave your baby behind.
Adoption is a wonderful choice
It gives families a chance to rejoice.
Adoption is something to be grateful for
It is an option one should not ignore.
If the choice was not adoption
I'm afraid termination would be the other option.
Thankful I must be
That termination was not chosen for me.

Joan Battilana

A Search to my Beginning

**Adoption makes one mother happy, yet the one mother sad
It gives a child a life she may never have had.**

Joan Battilana

HAPPY FATHER'S DAY!

I am so glad
You are my dad.
You work so hard and make me proud
I tell the world and I say it loud.
I love you more than **silver** and **gold**
It has to be said it has to be told.
Thank you Dad for choosing me
DAD to me is who you will always be.
I honor you Dad on this Father's Day
You brighten my life in your special way.
Thank you Dad for all you have done
You are the greatest Dad under the sun.
I LOVE YOU DAD!

Joan Battilana

A Search to my Beginning

Thank you Dad for choosing me.
DAD to me is who you will always be.

Joan Battilana

A Search to my Beginning

MY MOM

My mom is very loving and kind
A mother like her is hard to find.
I am so grateful she chose me
Without her I can't imagine where I'd be.
I know I can always count on her
She makes my days seem so much brighter.
Mom is my friend who will always care
Through thick and thin she is there.
I have learned a lot from her
To bake, to love and to have laughter.
God has played an important part
He gave my mom a great big heart.
Thankful I am for my mom's love
It fits my heart just like a glove.
No one will ever take her place
I am her daughter by God's grace.

Joan Battilana

A Search to my Beginning

**THANKFUL I AM FOR MY MOM'S LOVE
IT FITS MY HEART JUST LIKE A GLOVE.**

Joan Battilana

A Search to my Beginning

THIS MOTHER'S DAY

This Mother's Day is not like the rest
This year will be the best.
A baby girl was born years ago
To a young woman who had to let go.
Years have passed, Mother's Days have gone by
Remembering the girl often made her cry.
Her sons remembered Mother's Days in the past
But this year there is something to broadcast.
The girl that was raised by others
Found this woman and her brothers.
Complete this Mother's Day will be
Just look in her eyes and you will see.
Friends we have become, friends we will stay
Thank God for this special Mother's Day!

Joan Battilana

A Search to my Beginning

*This Mother's Day is not like the rest
This year will be the best.*

Joan Battilana

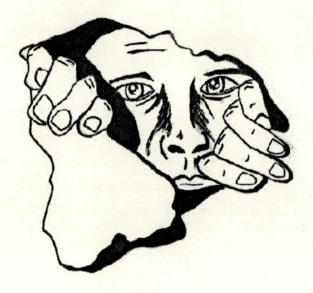

A Search to my Beginning

HE NEVER KNEW

He received a phone call late one night
"You have a daughter who has been out of sight".
A familiar voice was on the line
A girl he dated back in fifty-nine.
"I had a baby girl, forty years ago
I never told you, I didn't want you to know.
You were going your way and I went mine
A baby was not in our time line.
The decision I made for her was adoption
God answered my prayers and gave me that option.
This grown girl searched and found me
She wants to know who her father would be."
He hung up the phone in total despair
"What do I do now, am I supposed to care?
I've had a good life; I've been a horseman
I had a wife and several other children.
What would I have done if I had known?
Taken her in and called her my own?"
He never knew
What is he supposed to do?

Joan Battilana

A Search to my Beginning

He never knew
What is he supposed to do?

Joan Battilana

A Search to my Beginning

OUR BLENDED FAMILY

Our blended family is quite unique
We were all brought together by God's technique.
The first two adopted, the next two natural
We all grew up blessed and truly thankful.
Adoption gave my brother and I,
A life we will never deny.
My two sisters were born bright and beautiful
And for all this I am grateful.
The four of us have had our ups and downs
Lots of smiles and many frowns.
Siblings quarrel and siblings fight
Apparently we were born with that right.
Mom and Dad kept us all together
Knowing we'd be a family forever.
Genes play an important role
But not as important as what's in one's soul.
God set our foundation from up above
To be carried out by our parents' love.
Mom and Dad did not show favor
Each one of us special with our own behavior.
It is not easy for a family to blend
We've had our moments, we cannot pretend.
The love that started from the top
Will grow in this family and never stop.

Joan Battilana

Our blended family is quite unique
We were all brought together by God's technique.

Joan Battilana

"FAMILY BY CHANCE"

Years have gone by and who would have known,
Somewhere out there was one of our own.
Fate has brought us together,
Blood holds us forever!
We are a "family by chance" and will become "friends by choice."
What a day......we can all rejoice!
We all appear different by the way we were raised,
Our similarities have us amazed!
Forty years have come and gone,
We never had those years together playing on the lawn
Or telling secrets or sharing a song.
It is never to late...
Days, weeks and years will go by,
Families are always there to LOVE, laugh and cry.
No road is too long, nor city too far
We can pick up the phone or drive in our car.
Families are always nearby and we can never deny.
That we are a "FAMILY BY CHANCE"
and will become "FRIENDS BY CHOICE!"

Joan Battilana

A Search to my Beginning

We are a "family by chance" and will become "friends by choice."

Joan Battilana

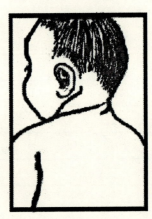

DIFFERENT

We are so different, can't you see?
I want to be able to be just me.
Raised together as a family for many years
I always wondered why I had all the fears.
Different we are as night and day
It's hard to know why, it's hard to say.
I wanted to be alone most of the time
You all went your way and I went mine.
Something was always missing to me
Even though God meant our family to be.
I was the one adopted many years ago
Genes we were born with made us different you know?
We cannot change what God has put together
We are a family with differences that will last forever.
Life lessons and values our parents put into place
Personalities and attitudes are genes we cannot erase.
Differences between us should not be a concern
Acceptance of each other is a value we must learn.

Joan Battilana

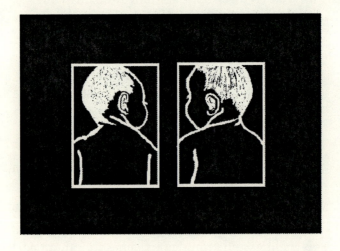

A Search to my Beginning

Different we are as night and day
It's hard to know why, it's hard to say.

Joan Battilana

A Search to my Beginning

"THAT BIG BROTHER OF MINE"

Situations separated us some forty years ago,
But time can never erase the love that is meant to grow.
The phone rang early one September morn,
A big brother on the other line seemed very torn.
"I really have a sister,
All these years, I have really missed her.
I did not know how to find you
I never knew what to do."
We laughed and we cried
Our childhood together had been denied.
He had his life and I had mine
All this we knew was in God's timeline.
Many differences but more similarities.
He loves the country and I love the city.
He has a dog and I have a kitty.
We both have blue eyes and blonde hair
We have so much to compare.
I have always wanted a big brother to call my own,
To approve of my boyfriends or help me get a loan.
We both agree it is never to late
To bring back the years and start a new slate.
This is the beginning of our life as big brother and sister
Nothing will keep us apart, not even a twister.
Now, when I see the sunshine,
I will always think of "That Big Brother of Mine!"

Joan Battilana

*Now, when I see the sunshine,
I will always think of "That Big Brother of Mine!"*

Joan Battilana

A Search to my Beginning

MY LITTLE BROTHER

All your life you've had an older brother.
Did you know you had another?
You also have an older sister
You never knew to miss her.
Adoption separated us years ago
You stayed and I was meant to go.
A family raised me to be their own,
You had a family that you've always known.
Would it have been different if I had been by your side?
I could have watched you and been your guide.
We can only imagine what it would have been like
To have played together or shared a bike.
When we met I was 40 and you 39.
We had lots to talk about in just a short time.
You had many memories to share.
I let you know I would always be there.
No one can change what has happened in the past
We can only go forward now and make memories that last.
You will always be a little brother to me
And I truly will be a big sister to thee.

Joan Battilana

A Search to my Beginning

You will always be a little brother to me
And I truly will be a big sister to thee.

Joan Battilana

A Search to my Beginning

"SISTERS BY CHANCE"

Years have gone by and who would have known,
Somewhere out there was one of our own.
Fate has brought us together,
Blood holds us forever!
We are "sisters by chance" and will become "friends by choice."
What a day......we can all rejoice!
We all appear different by the way we were raised,
Our similarities will have us amazed!
Forty years have come and gone,
We never had those years together playing on the lawn
Or telling our secrets or sharing a song.
It is never to late...
Days, weeks and years will go by,
Sisters are always there to LOVE, laugh and cry.
No road is too long, nor city too far
We can pick up the phone or drive in our car.
Sisters are always nearby and we can never deny
That we are "SISTERS BY CHANCE"
and will become "FRIENDS BY CHOICE!"

Joan Battilana

A Search to my Beginning

*Sisters are always nearby and we can never deny
That we are "SISTERS BY CHANCE"
and will become "FRIENDS BY CHOICE!"*

Joan Battilana

OUR BABY
(dedicated to my grandsons; Seth and Braxton)

The gift of a child is sent from above
Given to us to fill them with love.
All things happen in God's timeline
This baby is a blessing and it's yours and mine.
The love we have for each other will grow and grow
Our baby will feel that love and it will show.
Nine months and counting we can hardly wait
When our baby arrives we can all celebrate.
We pray our baby will be healthy and bright
God will provide and it ALL will be right.

Joan Battilana

The gift of a child is sent from above
Given to us to fill them with love.

Joan Battilana

A Search to my Beginning

'REUNION DAY'

The reunion day was fast approaching
I was in such a daze I could not keep track,
Clothes to iron and bags to pack.
Questions were dashing through my mind,
Would I look like her, was she kind?
Will I find her in a crowd?
Would she see me, would I make her proud?
The day arrived and off I went
Miles away to discover years unspent.
The plane landed and there I sat
Wondering want would come next, I didn't know the format.
Off the plane I went, nervous as can be
And then I saw her she looked just like me.
We ran to each other, we cried and we stared
There was so much to be shared.
I was not sure exactly what to say,
because…
We waited forty years for this Reunion Day!

Joan Battilana

A Search to my Beginning

We waited forty years for this Reunion Day!

Joan Battilana

I'M GLAD I FOUND YOU

I'm glad I found you!
At first I did not know what to do.
Adopted was a word I grew up with
My parents raised me as their own and that's no myth.
I always felt I was missing part of me
It's hard to explain, it's hard to see.
I decided to search and hopefully find
A part of me that has been hidden in my mind.
And then the day came, my search ended
I found my birth family and we all blended.
I see me in all of you
The parts that were missing are no longer an issue.
I now see why I do and say
It's from the genes I was given on my birthday.
I'm glad I found you
I now know what to do.

Joan Battilana

A Search to my Beginning

*I'm glad I found you
I now know what to do.*

SOME THOUGHTS TO REFLECT UPON

Make your inner most dreams realities.

Decisions are thought processes that affect not only yourself but also others.

The life of a child is precious and should be well-planned.

Fears are not realities.

Face your fears head-on.

The one thing you get out of life is experience.

Look at regrets as life's learning tools.

Your life is God's gift to you. The gift you give back to God is what you do with your life.

A Search to my Beginning

Dear Reader,

When you read poetry you have to process it, internalize it, and make it personal. Reflection is a big part of this internalization. I hope you will use the reflection pages for this purpose, thus making the poems more meaningful to you. Please let me know what you think about the poems and what they have meant to you. If you feel comfortable, please share your personal experiences with me about your adoption journey. I look forward to hearing from you. My email address is: jblueyes02@netscape.net.

Love,
Joan

Joan Battilana

Reflections

A Search to my Beginning

Reflections

Joan Battilana

Reflections

Reflections

Joan Battilana

Reflections

A Search to my Beginning

Reflections

Joan Battilana

Reflections

Reflections

Printed in the United States
883900004B